SEASONS IN THE SUN

Seasons in the Sun

Annest Gwilym

First published in: 2023

ISBN: 978-1-84527-938-7

Published with the financial support of the
Books Council of Wales

Cover design: Eleri Owen

Published by Gwasg Carreg Gwalch,
12 Iard yr Orsaf, Llanrwst, Wales LL26 0EH
tel: 01492 642031
email: books@carreg-gwalch.cymru
website: www.carreg-gwalch.cymru

For Isabella and Cara

Thanks are due to the following literary journals in which versions of some of these poems were first published:

Amaryllis
Black Nore Review
Clear Poetry
Culture Matters
Fevers of the Mind
Poetry Life and Times
Poetry Space
Reach Poetry
Red Poets
The Dawntreader
The Journal
The Poetry Kit
Ygdrasil

Contents

Seasons in the Sun

She lived in a net-curtained house
with anaemic pot plants and china figurines
of big-eyed animals and ladies in long dresses.
There was always the smell
of stale sponge cake and a scattering
of doilies, a brown flowered carpet,
drab furniture with crochet antimacassars.

She only spoke the island Welsh,
always with a twinkle in her eye.
We were no angels: girls that slipped
melting ice lollies through the dark mouths
of post boxes, stuck out our tongues
at strangers, danced the can-can
in her bloomers and best chapel hat
rummaged from her bedroom
while she spoke to our mother.

In a hot summer that reverberated to the sound
of roller skates tearing up concrete
she took us in her shiny black Morris Minor,
speeding past farms and fields of potatoes,
to the candy floss paradise of Benllech
with its wide apron of sand and donkeys.
Me in my beloved yellow towelling hot pants,
while "Seasons in the Sun" played
from everyone's open door.

Rhosmeirch '71

Endless days awash with sun and bees,
yellow flowers towered over me on the path
to the witch's house in the woods.

The musical box with its stiff, pink plastic ballerina
played *Swan Lake* as my father's home-brewed beer
burped its yeasty smell into the kitchen.

There were mountains jagged as teeth,
purple with heather and distance,
viewed from the sunny bay window seat.

The road to chapel was sweetened by wild strawberries –
an intense explosion on the tongue,
gritty, brimful with summer.

But one windy day at the end of August
I found our missing cat sprawled in a ditch,
her glossy suppleness collapsed to a popped balloon,
her face an ugly rictus and grimace of death.

Always in Lavender

Great Aunt May lived on the road to the beach
in a small Welsh fishing village.
Buck-toothed as a donkey, whiskery,
her home was a cabinet of wonders
for us children, spending summer holidays
in our grandfather's house next door.

Said to be unmarried because of
a desperate love for local poet Cynan,
she was the smartest woman in the village.
Clothes from Bon Marché in Pwllheli –
with matching shoes, hat and gloves –
worn with pride each Sunday to chapel.

In the front parlour, her glass cabinet
held all kinds of marvels –
sugar cubes in a crystal bowl
and silver tongs to handle them.
China lion ornaments guarded
each side of the mantelpiece.

She never looked at the painting of *Salem*
in the back parlour, ominous to me –
the Devil's face hidden in the crook of the arm
of the well-dressed, Welsh-hatted Siân Owen
in chapel, proud of her elaborate shawl,
oblivious to the sin of vanity.

The Sea Captain's Daughter

I was the sea captain's daughter
raised on tales of rounding the Horn,
the interminable blue vastness of oceans,
in a house full of Orientalia –
Chinese vases, carved wooden fishermen,
delicate cork landscapes in lacquered cases.

My soul was a poet's, a poet my love.
A distant ship on the horizon,
he sailed past me, parting the waters.
The enormity of night
and day's bright, white dome
brought him no closer.

With pinched lips I taught my class
about him; no other would do
so I filled my house with finery –
velvet drapes the colour of twilight,
beeswaxed parquet flooring,
the best crystal and china.

As winter comes again,
his death early in the year,
I am left with cavernous nights,
white mornings of mist and desolation,
my love a well-thumbed volume
marked 'Cynan' on the shelf.

Rose-Tinted

Those were days when the glitter
of stars fell onto my hair

As I unzipped the sky
allowing silence to speak

Shivery drops of soft rain
caught the silver of moonlight

Luscious streams of breeze
ruffled spider's webs, and me

Blood bubbled, fizzed under
the opium of his presence

A curve of coast, green sky-
stained reached into my past

The indigo pollen-light
glaze of sea pierced

Printed itself on my mind
stayed there and seared

Drifting draughts of days
each better than the last

The Greenhouse

At the top of the field
a room of wood and glass
that holds wonders.

Air heavy with earth and growth,
sun-born globes red as rubies
hang like baubles.

They leave a tang on the hands
and juice down the chins
of little thieves –

pick the bottom ones or those
hidden behind sticky leaves,
the smallest are the sweetest.

Grown by hands calloused
with use, earth-furrowed:
my grandfather's green thumbs.

Wraiths of Winter

Tenderly night creeps on silent feet
early, as if day were too weak to break;
sea glaucous as if full of spilt milk,
secrets spiralling in its depths,
surface still and opaque as opaline glass,
but with myriad life dancing beneath.

Ghosts are here where fog-haunted land
and water become one; the somnolence
of dense cloud canopy hides sun and moon.
Ghosts of long-gone sailors like those
who lived in my old sea captain's house,
where children were packed to the rafters.

Sometimes I see my great-grandfather –
who first went to sea here a boy of twelve –
eyes bright with adventure.
Away from his Llŷn home for the first time,
on a ship with a grey slate cargo –
stone gouged from the hearts of old mountains.

Soon they will build new sea defences,
so the water won't slop to our doorsteps.
Through the wraith-laden bay window
I dimly glimpse visions of rising,
shifting brine, changing the map of the coast:
a watery future wreathed in mist.

Winter's Breath

Winter's breath is snow-dust prophecy,
humus and moss-scented ache
of leaf mould from autumn on the floor.

Under the cold, clear fire of stars
its wind corrugates the sea's iron
in the silent meadows of the night.

Winter's woods are antlered, dark,
fox-sharp, full of long, wolfish shadows
that follow you home.

Its eye is pale, glaucous; air salted
with frost, whose sharp proboscis
probes every crack and crevice.

Winter is a black and white country.
The old know this: it strips flesh
from trees, flowers, bones.

Fair Maids of February

Necks arched like swans,
their flickering leaves scull
the frost-fringed moss,
last year's rain-gnawed leaves
where the bright beaks
of blackbirds stab and scour.

They form a chill flotilla on the hill
beneath woods where winter-bare
trees scratch a colourless sky
and a watery sun sits
on the horizon
like an over-fed cat.

Their pure lamps
shiver in needling wind
where all is quiet apart from
the black squabble of crows.
Heralds, they bring in
the sharp green scent of spring.

Wasps' Nest

In the dark interior of the shed
where only night's voice speaks

the hours here are alive, urgent,
with a furious, red-hot buzz.

The paper globe, a palace
made of wood and saliva

contains an invisible seethe –
pollinators, drunk on nectar.

By spring the empire falls –
a mass of tissue in my hand.

Restoration

Near the nature trail where they built
an ugly new house, uprooting ancient oak,
the wounded earth is slowly healing.

Buddleia bushes climb the sides
of the abandoned building, offering
their violet candelabras to the sky.

Rosebay willowherb and red valerian frame it
while below we hear the steady grumble of cars,
above in trees wood pigeons bubble their song.

Bramble bushes in flower make the house
inaccessible, unreachable without injury,
like a fairy tale castle without a princess.

Green algae works its way up the windows,
which still have the manufacturer's stickers. Nearby,
meadowsweet broadcasts its scent of honeyed almonds.

I imagine that inside it a fat slice of summer sun
penetrates the window, highlighting dust motes
and the mould that is starting to take over the walls.

And in my dreams I see an acorn take root
in the basement, an oak pushing its strong limbs
though windows, crumbling the structure to dust.

Mermaid

I found a mermaid on the beach
wrapped in moon-ruin and fishing nets.
Out of the water her hooked eyes
were dull, her scales tarnished.

Her useless tail flip-flopped like a dying fish
while salt-rub chafed her pale breasts.
Her hair was tangled in plastic;
the searing sun had blistered her skin.

I tried to drag her back into the water,
a dead weight, but left her there
when her constant wails of anguish
spoiled my mood, jarred my nerves.

The Desolation of Holiday Homes

St. David's Day

Today, prime-location rooms
are flooded with lake-light:
jellied, wobbling on walls, unseen.

Dust motes are gilded in this house
that is empty for ten months a year,
furnishings damp, hearth full of ashes.

The horns of some dead animal
adorn the hallway, a creature's pelt
sprawls on the parquet floor.

Mirror-like windows – blind eyes,
blink as the sun plays Midas
with the sunset's colours.

A forgotten piece of cheese
in the fridge hardens
to the consistency of toenail parings.

Weeds choke the flower beds
of pale daffodils in a froth
of algae green, drowned lemon.

A crinkle of dry beech leaves
crusts the driveway,
carries the scent of decay.

Fog-weary faces of daisies
hide in the overgrown grass,
beaded with secret dew.

Worn mountains look on –
holding the aspirations of the ages –
with their many scars, slippage of scree.

Wales for Sale

I

Houses are cheap here
ideal for second homes or Skybnb
cash cows, in prime locations

Many of our new neighbours
are from the same place as us
a home from home

Their estate agents favour us
we're willing to pay more
no need to wait to sell

Change the house name into
an English one, Welsh language mail
straight into the recycling

Ridiculous, moribund language
like something a hobbit would speak
sounds like they're clearing their throats

Maybe we'll start a little colony
our friends are interested
turn it into Cheshire-on-Sea

II

I grew up in a seaside village
I can't afford to buy there now
house prices soaring

Local buyers outpriced
by those wanting second homes
buy to let, holiday rents

You'd think you were in England
in some neighbourhoods
the nicest ones, with the best views

I will look instead at the poor areas
down at heel, run down
far from sea and lakes

The Romans knew it, the strongest
always conquer, leave their mark
the defeated lose it all

Carbon

The sun as dead as a daffodil in October,
the pavement today has a sprinkling of coal
crumbled to a thousand black diamonds,
dropped from the coal man's sack on the way
to a neighbour who no longer has a name for it.

The wind as tight as a drum transmits winter
down the road, turning the sea's breast into
a ploughed field, shredding
the Welsh flags on the pub, the dragons
a couple of whirling dervishes.

The cold slate step cools my feet, relic
of a dead industry – gouged mountains
and age-old poverty from living on poor land.
To the south, closed coal mines pose as
an ugly scar, a toothless mouth, an empty hearth.

The faint tang of smoke from a coal fire is not from
the house of the man with a crumbling mind.
The blinds are drawn in the old man's house
as the keening wind faintly sighs
ffarwel, ffarwel, ffarwel . . .

Insomniac

dawn coughs light
streaks the headache skies
too early
back to sleep

today the milk-sour mother
of tomorrow
illuminates curtain edges
with dust flowers
too bright
too early

blackbird alarm calls fracture silence
turn over
back to sleep

in the young day light grows dense
arthritic clock hands
march on
come back night
back to sleep

the moon has lost its drapery
ghosted by brightness
white din
too early

hands that twist the bedsheets
check the clock
tick tock
turn over

light coughs sifts
through curtains
takes root
too bright
come back night

cars growl past
like the ebb and flow
of thoughts

wind-washed rain spatters
drums on glass
too much noise
too early
come back night

In the Immensity of Night

Things with invisible hands
unlatch the doors unseen

Creep on silent feet
around my floating bed

Tap their long, strong nails
on my wooden headboard

Whisper poetry in my sleep
which evaporates at dawn

A crinkle of leaves gathers
at the base of the bed

While the sea laps at my front door
lost and miles from home

Baby crabs with tiny pincers
knock, want to enter

The herons are watching
as gulls tear candy floss clouds

Outside is dangerous, static-filled
inside is better

I pull the duvet under my chin
I think I'll stay here

Last Night . . .

I dreamed my soul rose
from my body whitely

like a sea mist coming in
from the west, its slow coolness,

diaphanous dampness,
hovering over the lumpen land.

I left behind this place of bones,
numb flesh silent as snow,

the past that is always present
in heavy muscles and sinew

with their scent of damp earth,
pallid roots and annelids.

I fled from stars that implode
behind the eyes, loudness of blood

crashing, roaring in ears
into the softness of ozone.

I learned to wear the cold like a shawl –
cold, like death, can be an ally.

Red on Red

Inspired by *Le Lit Rouge*, Francis Gruber, 1944.

Red protects itself. No colour is as territorial. It stakes a claim, is on the alert against the spectrum. (Derek Jarman)

i.
outside the room where nothing is natural and a red bed
burns on terracotta tiles   rooks make jagged black nests in
trees   piercing the innocence of baby blue skies   while she
stretches   opens her legs in invitation or obstruction
sensible shoes and ankle socks to hey babe take a walk on the
mild side   counting sunbeams and sunglasses contemplating
train times   lunch times   the times they are a changing times
bacteria breeding on skin   whether she dares eat a peach
how best to navigate squalid subways   breathe don't breathe
look up look down   walk   run   the number of steps required
to reach the pareidolian blue portal on the wall and whether a
slide of big red lipstick in *Love in a Lift* would calm her down

ii.
although it's spring   autumn hides and multiplies in young
hazel nuts that quietly bud on branches and brush the
window with newborn sweetness while archangels sleep in
attics waiting for Christmas and she contemplates red   for
love   life   death   disquiet   ardour   angst   the knife held too
close to the flesh   the exquisite pain that flowers   blooms
and how trees bear witness as they always must to the red of
dawn splitting the sky while angels hide in leaves that flicker
like flames

And Lie Beneath

I thought I heard your call last night in sleep,
your spider's touch like lace upon my cheek.
I open doors in endless halls of loss,
where marble floors are sepulchred in dust.
In empty rooms a phone is ringing out,
its strident cries unheard lament in vain.
The naked window frames a tattered moon,
a lonely dog is barking far away.
At times in crowds I seem to see your face;
it fades, a frosty stranger's takes its place.
Relentless as the stars the cycles turn,
but still I wander winter's frozen wastes.
They say I must succumb to the belief:
we come and walk the earth and lie beneath.

On Finding an Edward VII Coronation Medallion on the Beach

When days were like coins
slipping easily through my fingers
I saw it, rinsed and tided,
an edge of gold on the beach.

Smaller than a penny,
rimmed and tanged with tarnish,
at first I thought *Celtic hoard* –
a hill fort overlooking the shore.

A spill of thoughts of fortune
tumbled; ended when I cleaned it
and it revealed two vague heads
of a King and Queen.

A coat of arms on the back –
the date 9 August 1902 –
blurred by the weight and grind
of a hundred years of tides.

Uprooted from the moon's pull,
dark-sided drag on the beach,
placed in a glass cabinet,
it will not decay, become ill or old.

This Is Not How It Was Meant to Be

To be near the sea was all I dreamed of
in the unforgiving city, with its broken glass.

I've drained this place dry,
wrung sunsets from a watercolour sky,

tried to wear the sea's drapes as a dress,
the moon's tulle as a veil.

The sharpness of spring chafes my skin
as gulls slice dishwater skies.

Alone, I watch as a polygamous duck
and his two wives land on burnished water.

Poor man's beach – choked by remnants
of a dead industry, and litter.

Tired old sun in a silent sky
above the stale, clichéd sea.

This is not how it was meant to be.

The Shady House

In a shady house by Bangor Pier,
you are forever picking up dust.
On a diet of tobacco, herbs and beer,
you live as you know you must.

You are forever picking up dust,
as flies thumb window panes.
You live as you know you must,
in the pall of old people's homes.

As flies thumb window panes,
you rustle up your spliff.
In the pall of old people's homes,
the Brylcreem perfects your quiff.

You rustle up your spliff,
as the sea slides slyly past.
The Brylcreem perfects your quiff,
you see the top of a mast.

The sea slides slyly past,
you are starting to get high.
You see the top of the mast,
as a ghost-ship slithers by.

You are starting to get high –
the guitar is your curvy girl!
A ghost-ship slithers by,
sails of sand, decks of pearl.

The guitar is your curvy girl –
she never answers back!
Sails of sand, decks of pearl,
who said you had a lack?

She never answers back,
with hips like froth on beer.
Who said you had a lack,
in a shady house by Bangor Pier?

The Word Collector

Almost invisible ghost,
she hunts the early morning air
for a sliver of dream
floating down from
a just open bedroom window,
a catch of words in her throat,
wild and untamed.

Moon-eyed tempest-chaser,
deep as midnight,
as you pass in the street
she'll sieve your thoughts
before they settle in your head
like river mud.

The soft murmuration of leaves
in glassy, backlit light
gathers in her mind
like the phantom faces
of the children she never had.

She scours the beach
for its salty trawl
of sea pottery and glass,
filleting words and histories,
panning for gold.

Words unfurl and are caught
in the curve of a shell,
the wind's semaphore
in pollen-rich grass,
the moon tangled in trees.

Magpie-hearted collector,
words can never capture
the surging gold of sunrise,
or twilight's indigo fall.

Blodeuwedd Does the Dishes

She stands at the kitchen sink,
fingers puckering in lukewarm water.
Her hair is as frothy as meadowsweet,
golden as broom, silky as sunlight.

A loaf slowly bakes in the oven,
its scent makes her stomach groan.
As she gazes towards the distant forest
a pheasant's rusty call startles her.

She bats away a sibilant wasp.
Her floral perfume is like a veil,
but her secret scent is desolation,
bright and sharp as gorse.

In spite of all her allure,
her bones are limestone,
her eyes are haunted houses,
her blood peaty mountain streams.

You were made for me, you're perfect,
so you must not go out when I'm not here.
She thinks only of the stranger in the meadow
that morning, with his full-moon eyes.

He had gazed at her with no wish to possess.
He seemed to hold a promise of unfettered days
as he turned a burnished dagger over and over
in his hand, its mirrored finish flashing.

At night she dreams of leaving this world
of oven and hearth, slicing the midnight air
as an owl, unseen, untamed, in silent joy,
where she is the forest, the earth in bloom.

A Surrealist's Living Room

The sofa is a baggy old elephant
batting away mosquitoes in the heat,
its roomy rump wrinkled and worn.

In its creases there is *bara brith*,
a silver sixpence, a magpie's haunted eye
and a WWII hand grenade.

The peeling leather veneer
reveals flat continents, created
before the world was round.
Dragons stalk the oceans between them.

The TV is a portal where you can revisit
your past lives, by a sly click of the remote.
This brings a flotilla of violet butterflies
into the room, showering powder
that smells of jasmine and salt.

The ghosts of long-dead sea snails
despondently circle the bowl of exotic shells –
their dismal moans make the dog howl.

The silk flower display conceals an owl –
its eyes are the brown centres of two
oversized daisies, which send esoteric
messages to the sea snail ghosts.

Outside the bay window birds crowd
on the windowsill to see the giant flowers,
smallest and chirpiest ones at the front.

Sunsets are caught in the hand-painted mirror
from Hungary, which returns them
bloodied and magnified to the waiting sky.

The rug isn't magic but it does let you
contact the dead when you place a glass on it,
making the neighbourhood cats
yowl for their supper.

The telephone sits smug in its cradle –
it can teleport you to your dream destination,
if you ask it nicely three times.
Nausea, confusion and disorientation
are the gifts for those it doesn't like.

Green ceramic tiles form a grid system,
so you can find the Pharoah's tomb,
where wonderful things and a curse await you.

And if you fall under the room's spell,
you will never be able to leave.

July

Each day there is less light,
more darkness, as shadows lengthen.
There is an unravelling in the sky
as clouds spool away to the north.

Fungi and moss now cover the stumps
of trees the council cut down,
once marked with a red cross,
which I wanted to scrub away.

In the nettle-sour alley weeds
are taking over while in the hedgerow
a foxglove-bright sweet wrapper
is tangled in a bramble bush.

Someone's car stereo startles me
and thumps its way down the road.
Another plastic drink bottle soon
joins others necklacing the curb.

I remember the gardens where there were
hundreds of lilac orchids but the car park
grass where a lone orchid grew last year
has been scalped, daisy heads decapitated.

Butterfly-filled buddleias tower above
like beautiful girls as I sidestep
the remains of someone's Chinese meal,
casually dumped on the roadside.

In tired July, I walk through tigered darkness
and light, as I have always done.

One Day in August

Soft summer rain shakes
the buddleia tree growing on
the corner of a run-down house, releasing
the sweet smell of lilacs, and dust.

A shrill breeze makes the cables
on the boat masts ring like bells –
an urgent, amorphous symphony
in the salt-sharp air.

Pink clouds at sunset –
Breathe, breathe in the air playing –
punters from the pub zig-zag up the hill,
waltz with wheelie bins.

Oncoming night blurs, erases
the sharp angles of buildings.
Like a television set just switched off,
the air crackles with static.

Thirteen Ways of Looking at a Seagull

Inspired by Wallace Stevens' *Thirteen Ways of Looking at a Blackbird.*

I
The world was born
From the point of light
In a seagull's pale eye

II
Beneath the sign
DON'T FEED THE SEAGULLS
The seagulls feed themselves

III
In the sea's deep crypt
Two oysters and a mussel
Dream of seagulls

IV
In the woods of confusion
The way out is marked
By a trail of seagull droppings

V
The sun plays Midas on the water
While two seagulls play Mars
Over a limp sandwich

VI
A flock of seagulls
And a raven
Is still a flock of seagulls

VII
In a castle's cobbled forecourt
A seagull and a collared dove
Hold court

VIII
When skies are violent
A seagull's muscular wings
Hold up moisture-rich clouds

IX
Killers from the egg
Each seagull knows
How to catch a pike

X
In a manor's formal gardens
Where a marble fountain tinkles
A seagull's cries are informal

XI

From a train's rectangular window
Seagulls chase after a plough
Like a sudden snow blizzard

XII

One of Braque's birds
Dreamt that in another life
He was a seagull

XIII

Alone on a beach, a child watches
As a dead seagull's wing flaps
Quietly in the breeze

Days Like This to Be Read as Honey

For the Child I Never Had.

I would give you:
the honeydrip of low sun on the horizon;
a cold that sugar-coats mountain tops,
collides cells and atoms;
all the tree-lined hours of your dreams;
a moonsuck and sunstruck
clock stuck at youth;
four seasons in a day.

In my witchery I would
line up jars of bright starshine
on your windowsill;
conjure Caravaggio days,
raining pomegranate seeds;
trap it all in amber.

And if you ever lived,
you could live it too.

Sometimes at Twilight . . .

Inspired by Helen Dunmore's *Glad of these times.*

I open my back door
to the high clean ozone of the tide,
when the chill small evening
clinks with sounds of crockery
from the beach-side bistro
and wine-hazed banter.

And I'm glad of cormorants
that dry their wings
on the jetty's end,
sloe-dark eyes of a surfacing seal,
plants that grow
despite the wind's salt charge.

Glad that in spite of poverty
there are watery days
of soft rain and poetry,
the past that is always present
beneath the surface of earth and our skin,
the lost graves of my peasant ancestors.

Glad of the balm this place brings
to a frightened rescue dog
who now calls it home,
for being able to stand on my step at night,
sniff the air like a fox,
for what the wind brings.

Notes

Page 23: the title is a contradiction of *Nid Yw Cymru ar Werth* (Wales Is Not for Sale), a movement which seeks to address the current second homes crisis, which threatens the Welsh language and culture, as well as making house prices rise to levels unattainable for many native people.

Page 25: in Welsh *ffarwel* means *farewell.*

Page 46: 'Killers from the egg' is from Ted Hughes's poem *Pike.*